The Life and Times of

GEORGE ROGERS CLARK

GENERAL
GEORGE ROGERS CLARK
FELIX W. de WELDON
A GIFT TO THE PEOPLE OF LOUISVILLE
BY THE HILLMAN-HOPKINS FAMILY

Mitchell Lane PUBLISHERS

P.O. Box 196 · Hockessin, Delaware 19707

state – 9/10 – 8.76

Titles in the Series

The Life and Times of

The Life and Times of

GEORGE ROGERS CLARK

Russell Roberts

Printing   1   2   3   4   5   6   7   8   9

Library of Congress Cataloging-in-Publication Data
Roberts, Russell, 1953–.
    The life and times of George Rogers Clark / by Russell Roberts.
        p. cm. — (Profiles in American history)
    Includes bibliographical references and index.
    ISBN 1-58415-448-9 (library bound : alk. paper) $\overset{B}{CLA}$
    1. Clark, George Rogers, 1752–1818—Juvenile literature. 2. Generals—United States—Biography—Juvenile literature. 3. United States. Continental Army—Biography—Juvenile literature. 4. Virginia—Militia—Biography—Juvenile literature. 5. Northwest, Old—History—Revolution, 1775–1783— 23922 Campaigns—Juvenile literature. 6. United States—History—Revolution, 1775–1783—Campaigns—Juvenile literature. 7. Frontier and pioneer life—Northwest, Old—Juvenile literature. I. Title. II. Series.
E207.C5R63 2006
973.3'3092—dc22   2005036808

ISBN-10: 1-58415-448-9   ISBN-13: 9781584154488

ABOUT THE AUTHOR: Russell Roberts has written and published nearly 40 books for adults and children on a variety of subjects, including baseball, memory power, business, New Jersey history, and travel. The lives of American figures of distinction is a particular area of interest for him. He has written numerous books for Mitchell Lane Publishers, including *Nathaniel Hawthorne, Thomas Jefferson, Holidays and Celebrations in Colonial America, Daniel Boone,* and *The Lost Continent of Atlantis.* He lives in Bordentown, New Jersey, with his family and a fat, fuzzy, and crafty calico cat named Rusti.

PHOTO CREDITS: Cover, p. 8—North Wind Picture Archives; pp. 6, 18, 23, 34—Library of Congress; p. 12—Sharon Beck; p. 42—Army Military.

PUBLISHER'S NOTE: This story is based on the author's extensive research, which he believes to be accurate. Documentation of such research is contained on page 47.
    The internet sites referenced herein were active as of the publication date. Due to the fleeting nature of some web sites, we cannot guarantee they will all be active when you are reading this book.

Profiles in American History

Contents

British General Henry Hamilton surrenders Fort Sackville to George Rogers Clark on February 25, 1779. The victory, perhaps the high point of Clark's career, was accomplished by guile, bravery, and daring by the Americans. According to legend, when Hamilton saw the real size of Clark's tiny force, he turned away in disgust.

CHAPTER
1

Critical Crossing

Groups of weary men stood outside in the freezing February weather, staring at the icy, shoulder-deep water in front of them. Some of them wobbled in the cold wind like dying leaves on a tree limb. The air seeped right through their damp leather clothes and settled in their bones, chilling them to their very core. They shivered and shook. Hunger pains gnawed at them. They had not had a good meal in weeks.

Some of them turned away from the frigid water. Teary-eyed, they looked at their companions. They spoke in low, croaking, halting tones.

I can't, many said. *I just can't. I can't cross through any more frigid water. I can't be wet and cold anymore. I've had it. I'm played out.*

Almost in unison, the men looked to the tall, lean, powerfully built red-haired man standing off to one side. What was he going to do? Was this it? Had they come all this way, sloshing nearly two hundred miles through mud and icy water, sleeping on the cold, damp ground, holding their rifles over their heads to keep the gunpowder dry, only to have to turn back now? Were they finished?

The red-haired man was George Rogers Clark. For the past several weeks he had led his little army of around 170 men, half of them

Clark's men waded across the Wabash River during their historic march of nearly 200 miles in February 1779. At one point a fourteen-year-old drummer boy with the army floated across the water on his drum, greatly amusing the bedraggled men.

French volunteers and many of the others American frontiersmen, from a settlement called Kaskaskia in the sparsely settled Illinois Territory to here, near another village, Vincennes (on the present-day border between Illinois and Indiana). Not far away was British-occupied Fort Sackville, which guarded Vincennes. Clark intended to recapture Vincennes. If he could, it would be a major victory for America in the Revolutionary War against England.

Vincennes had already been under American control once, but just a few months before, in December 1778, British forces under Lieutenant Colonel Henry Hamilton had come down from Detroit and recaptured it. Clark knew that if he had remained at Kaskaskia, Hamilton would strength his forces and eventually attack and crush him. Before that happened, Clark had decided to attack Hamilton—in the dead of winter, marching over miles of wet, chilly, flooded ground. Most likely, Hamilton would not be expecting an attack at this time of year.

Much more than the fate of Clark's tiny army was at stake. Clark was trying to defend the Northwest Territory, a vast, sprawling unsettled area that included the modern states of Illinois, Ohio, and Indiana. The British and their American Indian allies were coming down from Canada and attacking colonial settlements on the western frontier, particularly in Kentucky and Pennsylvania. By seizing control of the country from the British, Clark could assure that America held the crucial northwest.

If Britain held this territory, it could continue to launch attacks on American frontier settlements in Pennsylvania and Kentucky. The British could even come out of the west with a powerful army and strike General George Washington's Continental Army from one direction while another British force struck it from the other. If that happened, Washington would be trapped between them. He would have to surrender. The war would be over. America would be lost.

So yes, a lot was at stake here—perhaps the future of America as an independent nation.

Clark looked at his thin, half-starved, weak, and tired men. They had already marched all this way against overwhelming odds. How could he ask them to go one step further? How could they attack Fort Sackville in this condition?

Clark did not hesitate. They had come too far to stop. He splashed into the chilly water. "Follow me!"[1] he cried.

Slowly, his men followed. Either in groups or individually, they waded into the frigid water, guns held high. Men who were too weak waited and grabbed the arms and hands of stronger companions. Those who found it too difficult to move through the water clung to a tree branch or other floating object until others could grab them and help them across.

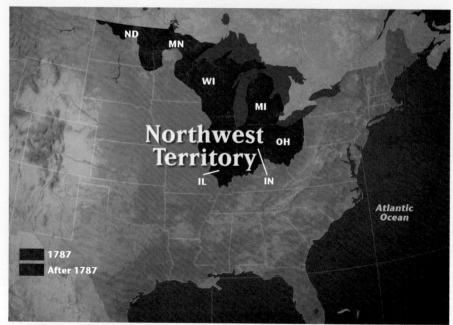

ND
MN
WI
MI
OH
Northwest Territory
IL
IN
Atlantic Ocean

1787
After 1787

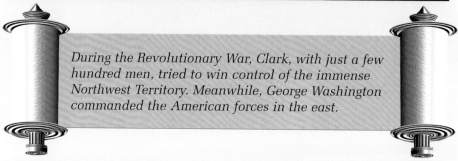

During the Revolutionary War, Clark, with just a few hundred men, tried to win control of the immense Northwest Territory. Meanwhile, George Washington commanded the American forces in the east.

Clark looked back and was pleased to see his men following him. But in what condition would they be when they got to Fort Sackville?

Clark did not know. All he knew was that he was betting everything on this gamble.

Who's In Charge?

It might seem odd today, when all states have firm boundaries, but during the American Revolution it was uncertain which states controlled which western territories. This led to a lot of confusion when it came time to defend those territories. For example, the region that today holds the Pennsylvania towns of Wilkes-Barre and Scranton was in dispute over who controlled it. Both Pennsylvania and Connecticut claimed ownership of the area. In 1775, Pennsylvania sent their militia to evict Connecticut settlers there. The Pittsburgh region was claimed by both Pennsylvania and Virginia. Settlers from both states poured into the area and set up rival court systems. Judges from each side arrested those on the other.

Virginia, biggest of the original thirteen colonies, had the largest and most distant western borders to defend. The colony's original charter was often interpreted as granting it all land to the west and northwest as far as the western ocean. In the case of Kentucky, Virginians had long had an interest in the area. In 1750 and 1751, Virginians Thomas Walker and Christopher Gist, both land company representatives, had been the first Englishmen on record to enter the area.

Thus Virginia claimed a large part of the western frontier: all of the present-day states of Kentucky, Illinois, Ohio, and West Virginia and part of Pennsylvania. However, the colony found it difficult to find resources to protect so vast a region.

Early settlers in those areas were often on their own, with no government assistance as far as defense against American Indian attacks. Since the land was in dispute between one or more colonies, the settlers had no one to whom they could appeal for help. Ironically, American Indians were often victimized by this same lack of authority. For generations, they had hunted and fished this land, and now it was being taken over. Sometimes people pretending to be in authority negotiated deals with the Indians for land—deals that were not legal and did nothing to stop the continued spread of colonial settlement. These deceitful dealings further angered the Indian nations and often led to more bloodshed.

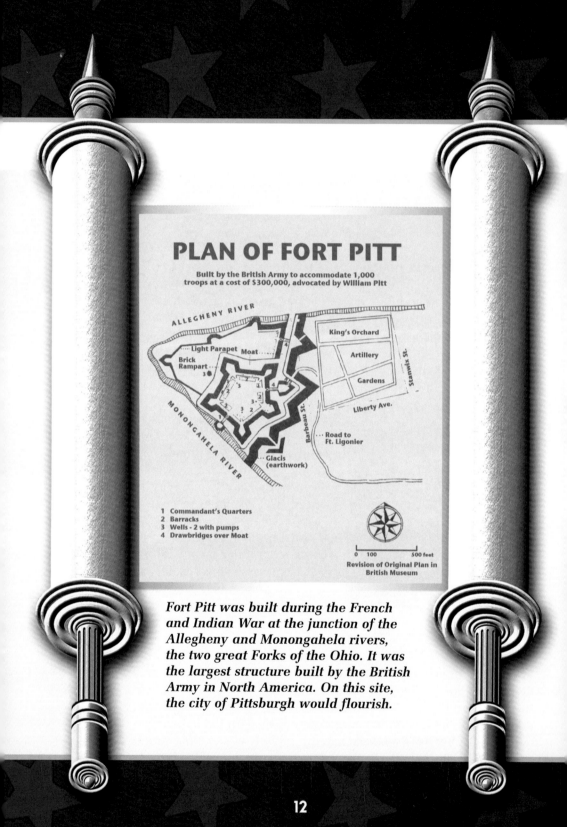

PLAN OF FORT PITT

Built by the British Army to accommodate 1,000
troops at a cost of $300,000, advocated by William Pitt

ALLEGHENY RIVER

Light Parapet   Moat

Brick
Rampart
3

MONONGAHELA RIVER

Glacis
(earthwork)

King's Orchard

Artillery

Gardens

Stanwix St.

Liberty Ave.

Barbeau St.

Road to
Ft. Ligonier

1 Commandant's Quarters
2 Barracks
3 Wells - 2 with pumps
4 Drawbridges over Moat

0   100   500 feet
Revision of Original Plan in
British Museum

*Fort Pitt was built during the French
and Indian War at the junction of the
Allegheny and Monongahela rivers,
the two great Forks of the Ohio. It was
the largest structure built by the British
Army in North America. On this site,
the city of Pittsburgh would flourish.*

12

CHAPTER
2

Early Life

George Rogers Clark was born on November 19, 1752, in Albemarle County in Virginia, near Charlottesville. He had red hair when he was born. According to a family tradition, redheaded Clarks always distinguished themselves. His father was John Clark and his mother, Ann Rogers, became Ann Clark at fifteen. She was John Clark's cousin. Three miles away and eight years earlier, the red-haired Thomas Jefferson had been born.

In 1757, the Clark family moved east, to a plantation in Caroline County, Virginia. George and his older brother, Jonathan, went to a school run by Donald Robertson. James Madison, who would become the fourth U.S. president, was also a schoolboy there. Supposedly, Robertson sent George back to his parents with a message that it was a waste of money to try to educate him. Even so, going to school gave George a lifelong love of books, particularly history and geography. He received some military training from a man named George Muse, who reportedly also taught George Washington. Clark's grandfather, Jonathan Clark, taught him surveying.

In April 1772, at not yet twenty years old, Clark left home to strike out on his own. His family now included five brothers and four sisters. By early June he was at Fort Pitt (Pittsburgh), floating down the Ohio River through country that was so sparsely settled that he passed only one other colonial settlement. Clark, however, fell in

love with the area. When he returned home, he talked so enthusiastically about the land that his father became excited too. The two planned a return trip.

In late summer or early autumn of 1772, Clark, his father, and four others set out. About forty miles below Wheeling, Virginia, George settled alongside Fish Creek and planted corn. His father returned home. By this time, other settlers were streaming into the area. Clark was in great demand as a surveyor. Between jobs, he made several trips back to his parents' home. By September 1773, the once thinly settled country had new settlements 350 miles below Fort Pitt.

These new settlements displeased the American Indians, who found the colonists slowly pushing them off their land. Attacks between the two sides were common.

By this time, Clark had undoubtedly heard about a magnificent new country to the west of Virginia—a place where the game was abundant and the land rich and fertile. It also had no Indian villages. The Shawnee and the Cherokee used it as their hunting ground, but no tribes called it home. The place was Kentucky, and its siren song would soon draw many settlers to it, including a hunter and trapper named Daniel Boone.

On May 14, 1774, Clark received his first military commission as a militia captain. For the next few months he served in a campaign against the Shawnee Indians known as Lord Dunmore's War. The Battle of Point Pleasant (in present-day West Virginia) in October 1774 ended with the defeat of the Shawnee. Toward the later part of that year, Clark was involved in Indian peace talks.

The Shawnee defeat was a signal that the western frontier was safe, and the area was soon swarming with settlers. Early in 1775, Clark was hired by the Ohio Company as a deputy surveyor working in Kentucky. The more he saw of Kentucky, the more he liked it. Kentucky land, he wrote to one of his brothers, was "as good as any in the World."[1]

Meanwhile, another war had erupted—this one between the American colonies and England. The Revolutionary War began in April 1775 with fighting at Lexington and Concord. This news, combined with the continued unhappiness of the Shawnee and Cherokee, made settlement of Kentucky still risky. However, in September 1775, the families of Daniel Boone and others came to Kentucky to make their home. Others soon followed.

For the settlers, there were problems. Individual Kentucky land claims were being swallowed up by larger claims, like that of Richard Henderson and his Transylvania Company. Henderson had claimed practically all of Kentucky in an attempt to establish a new American colony called Transylvania. This gigantic claim threatened many of the individual claims Clark had laid out, including his. Disputes erupted between people with conflicting claims. Kentucky the paradise threatened to become Kentucky the battlefield.

In the autumn of 1775, Clark went to see the Virginia government in Williamsburg (since Virginia was thought to be in charge of Kentucky) to find out whether Henderson's claim was legal or not. He found some who thought Henderson's claim was legal. Others had doubts. Clark decided to arrange an election of Kentucky deputies by popular vote to go to Williamsburg and settle the confusing matter in legislative session. Even more important, Clark was hoping to establish a firmer connection between Kentucky and Virginia. He wanted recognition of Kentucky as a Virginia county, which would give the area greater protection from Indian attacks. If this failed, he wanted Kentucky to become independent.

Establishing the area's status was the purpose of a meeting Clark called with members of other Kentucky settlements at Harrodsburg, perhaps the most important Kentucky community, on June 6, 1776. He called the meeting on his own authority, but when others heard that it was Clark who had called the conference, they willingly attended—a sign of how much he was respected. At the meeting, he and John Gabriel Jones were elected delegates to the Virginia legislature on behalf of Kentucky. A few days later, the two men set out for Williamsburg.

The trip was an exercise in agony and terror. Jones's horse gave out, forcing the two to use one animal. It was rainy and damp, which soaked their feet inside their moccasins. They dared not light a fire at night to dry the soggy shoes for fear of Indians. The constant rubbing of their wet skin on the wet leather of their shoes caused the two men to come down with what frontiersmen called scald feet—a condition that caused the skin to become inflamed and turn an angry red, making every step agony.

With the sounds of Indian rifles all around them, Clark and Jones made a desperate decision. They decided to rest their feet at an abandoned cabin called Martin's Fort. They knew they could be easily discovered and overwhelmed by Indians in the tiny cabin, but it was a risk that Clark knew they must take if they were to have any hope of reaching Williamsburg.

The gamble paid off. The men soothed their sore feet with a poultice, then continued safely on to Williamsburg. When they arrived, they found that they were too late for the assembly's session, so they separated. Jones headed for North Carolina. Clark, however, went to Virginia governor Patrick Henry's home to plead Kentucky's cause.

From his sickbed, Henry listened to Clark. Much impressed, he sent Clark off to a legislative council of the assembly with his support. Clark presented Kentucky's case, but the council was not as impressed as Henry. They gave Clark 500 pounds of gunpowder for defense, but told him he would have to find some way of getting it back himself, since Kentucky was not officially part of Virginia.

Clark fumed. Kentucky had helped Virginia by protecting its western frontier; now the Virginia government was turning its back on it. Furious, Clark refused the offer of the gunpowder and proclaimed: "If a country was not worth protecting it was not worth claiming."[2] Kentucky, he hinted, would look elsewhere for protection.

Clark's implied threat worked. The council quickly paid to have the gunpowder sent to Fort Pitt. Clark wrote to friends in Kentucky to make arrangements to retrieve it.

Now Clark and the recently returned Jones went before the autumn session of the assembly to ask that they declare Kentucky a county of Virginia. They were opposed by Richard Henderson, who knew that the designation would ruin his plans for Transylvania. However, Clark's arguments, with the support of Patrick Henry and Thomas Jefferson, were stronger. On December 7, 1776, the assembly voted to admit Kentucky as a Virginia county.

When Clark returned to Fort Pitt on his way back to Harrodsburg, he found the 500 pounds of gunpowder still there. He and several others tried to bring the powder down the river. They were chased by Indians. Clark finally decided to hide the gunpowder on land, then go back for it later. Eventually others were able to go back, retrieve the much-needed gunpowder, and transport it to Harrodsburg.

The first couple of months in 1777 at Harrodsburg were quiet ones. Clark wrote in his diary, "Nothing Remarkable done."[3]

Little did he realize how quickly things would change.

Transylvania in America?

Monster movie fans know that the vampire Count Dracula lives in Transylvania, a region that is now part of Romania. But did you know that there was once a Transylvania in America?

The word *Transylvania* means "beyond the forest"—in other words, in the yonder frontier. The Transylvania Company was a land company formed by Richard Henderson to colonize much of what are now the states of Kentucky and Tennessee when those areas represented the frontier.

Henderson was born in Virginia in 1735. In 1768 he became a judge with the Superior Court of North Carolina. He retired from the court in 1773 to pursue land colonization. In 1774 he formed the Louisa Company, which became the Transylvania Company in January 1775. He made a treaty with the Cherokee Indians for 17 million acres—an enormous amount of land—in what are now Kentucky and Tennessee.

Daniel Boone travels Wilderness Road

Among those he interested in his new venture was an American frontiersman named Daniel Boone. Henderson hired Boone to blaze a road to the new territories. Called the Wilderness Road, it was more than 200 miles long. It went from western Virginia through eastern Tennessee, through the Cumberland Gap, and into central Kentucky.

In May 1775, Henderson called a meeting of representatives from various Kentucky settlements. They petitioned the Continental Congress to recognize the colony of Transylvania and give it equal status with the other thirteen colonies. Congress ignored the petition. In December 1776, Virginia took over the whole region as a county, further hampering Henderson's dreams.

After the Revolutionary War ended, Henderson's claim was declared meaningless. He later was involved in settling western Tennessee. He died in 1785.

For Your Information

Clark's force attacks Fort Sackville in February 1779. By varying his gunfire from heavy to light, Clark confused the British inside the fort as to how many men he really had with him.

CHAPTER
3

Long Knives

A little after Clark wrote those words, from far-off London came an order: British commanders in America, finding the American army and its leader, George Washington, tougher than they thought, were to arm the Indians and use them as allies against the colonials. The British would supply weapons. They would encourage the Indians to attack frontier settlements, such as Harrodsburg, Kentucky.

The Indians needed hardly any encouragement. They had been trying to get the settlers out of Kentucky for some time. Already Shawnee warriors had attacked Harrodsburg in early March 1777, trying to drive the settlers away. They then continued the attacks so that the Harrodsburg citizens could not plant any corn that year. All they had to eat were turnips. Conditions at the other Kentucky settlements were not much better. Once the British began arming the Indians, the outlook for the settlers grew even worse.

On March 5, 1777, Clark was promoted to a major of the Virginia militia and put in charge of Kentucky's defense. He was just twenty-four years old.

Clark thought that if he could control the vast Illinois country, the Indians would no longer be able to use it as a springboard from which to attack Kentucky, and the British could not occupy it. It seemed like an impossible dream—there were not enough troops to defend Kentucky, let alone go on the offensive in faraway Illinois—but if it

worked it would probably save Kentucky. On October 1, 1777, Clark went to Williamsburg to see Patrick Henry. Virginia's support of Clark's operation was critical. He was counting on Virginia for men and money.

Governor Henry approved the plan, but he wanted to keep Clark's main purpose secret. All he would tell the Virginia General Assembly was that Clark was to get money and men to help defend Kentucky. He did not reveal that Clark intended to do that by leading a daring expedition to attack British frontier outposts in the Illinois country. Henry also promoted Clark to lieutenant colonel.

Over the next few months, Clark recruited about 150 men. Many of them were frontiersman who had been nicknamed "long knives" by the Indians because of their long hunting knives.

On May 12, 1778, the small force, along with a group of settlers, set out for the frontier, picking up a few more troops along the way. Only a few officers knew the real purpose of the mission. As Patrick Henry told Clark: "You are to take especial care to keep the true destination of your force secret. Its success depends upon this."[1]

The tiny army rode the Ohio River to the Falls of the Ohio, a two-mile stretch of rapids. Clark went into camp on Corn Island. There they established Fort Nelson, considered the forerunner of the modern city of Louisville, Kentucky. (Clark is considered the founder of Louisville).

At this point, Clark finally told his men of their real destination. Some of them did not like the idea; there was nothing in Illinois but Indians, British soldiers, and the French. About 50 men deserted, leaving him with around 180 overall. He was outnumbered 25 to 1 by hostile natives.

Nevertheless, Clark felt optimistic. On June 26, he and his men paddled through the Falls of the Ohio during an eclipse of the sun. Clark proclaimed the eclipse a good omen.

Clark and his small force advanced on Kaskaskia, in the Illinois territory. The community was primarily made up of French citizens overseen by a French soldier, even though it was under British rule. Before Clark could assault it, he received word that France had signed a treaty of alliance with America. He hoped that this would make taking Kaskaskia, with its large French population, easier.

Clark's force arrived just a few miles outside of Kaskaskia in the late afternoon of July 4, 1778. He decided on a night attack so that his men would have as much of an advantage as possible. That night Clark and his men slipped through the main gates of the fort that guarded the town. Incredibly, the gates were unmanned. Quickly the Americans made their way to the commander's cabin. A few minutes later, the French commander, the Chevalier de Rocheblave, awoke from a sound sleep to find a group of Americans surrounding his bed. He quickly surrendered. Kaskaskia had fallen without a shot.

Initially, Clark terrorized the town by making everyone stay inside. The French inhabitants feared the worst from the invaders, having heard of their fierce reputation.

Clark had a reason for initially causing fear. "I considered that the greater the shock I could give them in the beginning, the more appreciative they would be later of my lenity and the more valuable as friends,"[2] he said.

Suddenly pleasant, Clark told Father Pierre Gilbault, a representative of the townspeople, that the Americans had come as friends, not enemies. He also told him of the alliance between France and America. Overwhelmed by Clark's attitude, the townspeople immediately switched their allegiance from the British to the Americans. They even helped Clark capture Cahokia—another French settlement under British control fifty miles north of Kaskaskia—by telling the people of the kindness of the Americans.

Next Clark decided to take the village of Vincennes, near the present-day border of Indiana and Illinois. It was the last major outpost in Illinois. If the Americans could take it, the nearest British presence would be at Detroit, several hundred miles away.

Father Gilbault went ahead to talk to the largely French population of Vincennes. Once again, without firing a shot in anger, the community surrendered itself to Clark in August 1778. Captain Leonard Helm was sent to take charge of the fort there—Fort Sackville.

Now Clark had to deal with the Indian tribes in the area. They were still British allies, and if they ever rose up in unison against the tiny American army, they would certainly crush them.

As with everything else he had done so far, Clark had a plan. "I had always been convinced that our general conduct of Indian affairs was wrong," he said. "Inviting them to treaties was considered by them

in a different manner than we realized; they imputed [attributed] it to fear on our part, and the giving of valuable presents confirmed them in this opinion."[3]

Clark met with the Indians in late August at Cahokia. At the end of the first day's meeting, he refused to shake hands with the various chiefs present "until the heart could be given also."[4] What Clark meant was that he would not shake the chiefs' hands until he truly meant it. This impressed the Indians, for they had had many previous experiences with whites who had shaken hands and pretended to be their friend when they did not mean it.

The next day brought even more surprises for the Indians. Clark made a speech in which he told them they had two choices: war or peace. "Take whichever you please,"[5] he said.

Few whites had ever put matters so bluntly to the Indians before. The Indians chose peace. So completely had Clark won their confidence and friendship that, even years later, if he was at a council, he was the only white man with whom the Indians would speak. Clark had so far accomplished much of his plan.

At this point the British in Detroit, under the infamous "hair buyer" Lieutenant Governor Henry Hamilton (who reputedly paid for settlers' scalps), decided to reclaim the land lost to the Americans. On December 17, Hamilton's forces overwhelmed the tiny garrison left to defend Fort Sackville, and they recaptured Vincennes.

By the end of January 1779, Clark knew that Vincennes had fallen to the British. He also realized that Hamilton could use the town as a base to attack and reclaim the Illinois country.

Even worse, if Hamilton could unite the Indians in the region behind him, he would have a large and virtually invincible force. No one on the frontier would be a match for him. After laying waste to Illinois, he could go on to destroy the Kentucky settlements. Hamilton could head east with his army. He might even be able to menace George Washington's Continental Army from the west and trap him in a pincers movement with an eastern British force. If that happened, the Revolution would be lost; America would be defeated. There was only one thing for Clark to do about Hamilton: "I knew if I did not take him he would take me,"[6] he later wrote.

Moving swiftly, he bought a boat named the *Willing* and turned her into a tiny warship. Early in February the *Willing* sailed for

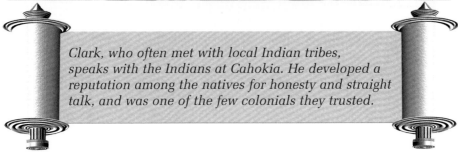

Clark, who often met with local Indian tribes, speaks with the Indians at Cahokia. He developed a reputation among the natives for honesty and straight talk, and was one of the few colonials they trusted.

Vincennes with about 45 men under the command of John Rogers. He was to position his command about 30 miles below Vincennes to cut off any escape by the British that way. On February 5, Clark and his men set off for Vincennes.

In front of them was a formidable journey. They had to cross 180 miles of flooded ground made slushy by winter rain and snow, and by rivers that had topped their banks. Yet Clark intended to

march to Vincennes, avoid the hostile Indians that appeared to be everywhere, and surprise Hamilton. It seemed impossible.

Clark and his men struggled to make good time in the awful conditions. No one had waterproof clothes, and the persistent rain and damp ground soon made everyone wet and miserable. At night they had to sleep on soggy ground.

Clark tried desperately to keep his men's spirits up. He sang songs, yelled out silly remarks, and kept saying that their destination was just ahead. He allowed his men to shoot at whatever game they encountered as they marched. Each night Clark turned dinner into a special occasion. The companies took turns inviting the others in the command to the meal. After eating there was dancing, singing, and a general spirit of gaiety. It may not have made the dampness and cold go away, but at least it helped the men forget them.

When the command reached the twin branches of the Wabash River on February 13, more trouble awaited them. The rains had caused a five-mile swamp between the two rivers to flood to depths of at least three feet. With little choice, Clark and his men crossed the chest-high water. They had to hold their guns above their heads to keep the gunpowder in them dry.

The men were cheered while crossing by the antics of a fourteen-year-old drummer boy. When the water got too deep for him, he floated across on his drum, greatly amusing the men. When he saw the effect he was having, the boy sang funny songs.

Soon Clark's men were in earshot of the cannon at Fort Sackville. On February 23, 1779, they began closing in on Vincennes.

Clark decided to use his already strong appeal among the French to send a message to the French citizens of Vincennes not to support the British troops inside the fort. In doing this, Clark was again taking a huge risk. The British garrison inside the fort might be alerted to his presence, thus spoiling the element of surprise that he had tried so hard to maintain. If the British should manage to contact their Indian allies, they could easily attack the rear of Clark's forces.

Clark used another trick to make his army seem larger to the townspeople of Vincennes. With flags waving, he marched his troops all around the fort, where they were largely hidden from view. The people kept seeing flags passing by, making them think he had many more men than he actually did.

Clark's message and trick worked. When his wet, cold, and hungry men entered Vincennes, they found many houses with their front doors wide open and hot food waiting on the table. The French citizens had decided to side with them.

Even while Clark was taking possession of the town, the fort remained blissfully unaware of his presence. That very day, the British soldiers at the fort had finished making some much-needed repairs to it. They had celebrated the end of those repairs by playing outdoor games. All of this had tired them out. As night fell, the weary men were resting.

Meanwhile another pleasant surprise awaited Clark. Captain François Bosseron, head of the French militia at the fort and who at the time was subject to Hamilton's orders, obviously had no love for the British. He had hidden a large supply of gunpowder when Hamilton had arrived, and he gave it to Clark. Much of the Americans' gunpowder was wet from the long, soggy march, and this supply of dry gunpowder was welcome.

That night, Hamilton sat down to an evening of card playing with his prisoner, the former American commander of the fort, Captain Helm. Outside, Clark and his men crept closer and closer to the fort. Several times he heard shots outside, but Hamilton continued with his game.

All at once there was a volley—numerous shots at once—and Hamilton could no longer avoid the truth. He was under attack. Helm warned the British troops running to their posts to stay away from the portholes cut in the fence for them to fire their weapons through, or they would have their eyes shot out. This dire prediction immediately demoralized the British soldiers.

Worse was to come. Clark's men poured heavy fire into the fort, then stopped, then started again. In the darkness, the confused British didn't know how many of the enemy was outside.

At nine o'clock on the morning of February 24, Clark tried a bold gamble before the British in the fort found out how few men he really had: He sent a note to Hamilton demanding his surrender. He made the first words sound as threatening as possible:

"Sir. In order to save yourself from the Impending Storm that now Threatens you I order you to Immediately surrender yourself up with all your Garrison . . ."[7]

Hamilton's icy reply was that the British Army was not in the habit of giving in to threats. Nevertheless, negotiations began between the two sides. Hamilton stalled for time, hoping that reinforcements would come. He asked for a three-day truce. Clark refused. The two sides were stalemated.

An Indian raiding party, sent out previously by Hamilton and unaware of what was happening, rode up to the fort. Clark's men captured several of them and dragged them out in full view of the fort. "I now had a fair opportunity of making an impression,"[8] Clark later said.

Clark made his impression. He had several Indians killed and their bodies thrown into the river before the horrified eyes of the British. Then Clark, covered in blood from the killings, casually washed the gore off his face and hands before walking up to the fort's gate to meet Hamilton to discuss surrender.

Realizing he was facing an enemy who would stop at nothing, Hamilton began earnestly negotiating surrender terms. Clark said that he would accept no terms other than unconditional surrender. When Hamilton asked why, Clark said that he intended to put to death any British soldiers who had helped stir up the Indians against the frontier. He named Major Jehu Hay, who was standing nearby, as one of those. Hay almost fainted.

The next day, February 25, 1779, Hamilton surrendered. According to legend, when Hamilton saw the true size of Clark's tiny army, he turned away in disgust, tears in his eyes.

At the age of twenty-six, George Rogers Clark had become famous as a champion of the American Revolution. With just a handful of brave men, he had overcome tremendous obstacles. He had stopped the British and Indians from laying waste to the frontier, and possibly from coming after Washington's men from the west. No greater hero existed at this time in America.

But fame is fickle.

The "Hair Buyer"

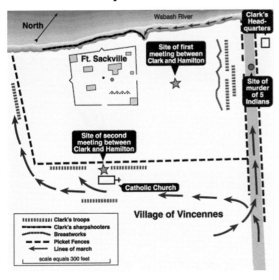

Henry Hamilton, the British commander at Vincennes who was defeated by George Rogers Clark, was greatly hated by Americans on the frontier.

Born in Ireland in 1734, Hamilton served with distinction in the British Army during the French and Indian War. In 1775, he became the lieutenant governor at Detroit. He maintained good relations with the Indians in the frontier territory. However, he was hated by Americans because he supposedly paid the Indians for every American scalp that they brought him, which obviously encouraged the Indians to attack settlers. Was this story true? It is uncertain, and many historians have dismissed it as a legend. Nevertheless, Hamilton became known in his day as the infamous "hair buyer," and this is how he has come down through history.

After his capture by Clark, Hamilton was sent to Williamsburg as a prisoner. Unfortunately, his "hair buyer" reputation had preceded him. Governor Patrick Henry put him in irons and had him thrown into a jail cell so unsanitary that it greatly affected his health.

At the time, prisoner exchanges between the Americans and the British were common. Hamilton's rough treatment so angered the British that they stopped exchanging American prisoners of war for British. Eventually, when Thomas Jefferson became Virginia's governor, he lessened the severity of Hamilton's treatment. Although Jefferson still would not grant him parole, Hamilton's relationship with Jefferson improved so greatly that he was often a houseguest of the governor's.

In March 1781, Hamilton was finally exchanged to the English for American prisoners. He later served as governor of Bermuda. He died in 1796.

Baron Friedrich von Steuben, who had been an officer in the German army, obtained a commission with the Continental Army. In February 1778, he trained Washington's troops at Valley Forge, Pennsylvania. Von Steuben commanded the force in Virginia in 1781, during Clark's only Revolutionary War battle in the east.

CHAPTER
4

Opportunity Lost

While the recapture of Vincennes was certainly important, Clark knew that the real power of the British in the northwest lay in Detroit. The downfall of Vincennes was a blow to British operations in the frontier; the downfall of Detroit might destroy them.

For a few days after the fall of Vincennes, Clark considered pushing on to Detroit. It was possible that the same tactics that had worked so far might also work at Detroit. From spies, Clark knew that Detroit's large French population was very unhappy under English rule and was near revolt. Captain Richard Lernoult, the British commander of Detroit, heard about Clark's victories and knew he was a likely next target. His force was small and ill-equipped. Clark had proven to be an able commander. It probably would not take him much to capture Detroit. Lernoult nervously appealed for assistance.

Wild rumors swept Detroit. Clark had 1,400 American troops, 600 French troops, and almost a dozen pieces of artillery. He was building boats in Milwaukee. Then he was in Chicago buying horses to aid in his attack. These were all rumors, but it showed how worried the enemy was about him

A story spread in Indian camps that a French fleet was coming to recapture all of Canada. The Indians were worried that they had picked the wrong ally in the war between the Americans and British. The Indians had become dependent on British supplies—

firearms, axes, blankets, and other goods. What would they do if the Americans kicked the English out of the northwest? How would they survive? What would the vengeful Americans do to them?

At that moment, Clark's way to Detroit was wide open, but he needed supplies for his men. He did what he had done before—he charged the supplies to the account of patriotic merchant Oliver Pollock in New Orleans and to the state of Virginia, certain that they would make good on the bills. For payment of many of the bills and expenses, he assumed personal responsibility. Little did he know, he would come to regret his actions.

Meanwhile, according to messages from Virginia, 500 men were on their way to him. Another report indicated that 300 Kentuckians under Colonel John Bowman were coming as well. The man whose victories had been a combination of bravery and boldness turned cautious. He decided to wait for the additional men.

However, the promised reinforcements did not arrive. Only 150 men from Virginia, not 500, finally showed up. As for the Kentuckians, instead of joining Clark, they went off to attack the Shawnee town of Chillicothe. The Shawnee had launched many attacks on Kentucky settlements from Chillicothe, and it was hoped that attacking the village would destroy the Shawnee's ability to harass the settlers. In the end, except for killing the Shawnee chief Blackfish, the raid was unsuccessful. Eventually most of the men returned home to Kentucky. Only thirty joined Clark.

By this time it was July 1779. The moment to attack Detroit had passed. The British had hastily and effectively rebuilt its defenses. The English—not Clark—had gotten stronger.

Clark knew full well that a golden opportunity had slipped through his fingers. "Never was a person more mortified than I was at this time," he said. "Detroit lost for the want of a few men."[1]

Just as Clark was abandoning his dreams of attacking Detroit, word came that Virginia had awarded him a special sword in honor of his victories. It was not a new sword, but a little-used sword that had belonged to someone else. Reportedly, Clark, already bitter at Virginia's lack of support with men and supplies, received the sword on the same day that a bill for supplies charged to Oliver Pollock came back disputed. In a silent fury, Clark stuck the sword into the ground, broke it in half, and kicked the top half into a river.

In September 1779, Thomas Jefferson succeeded Patrick Henry as Virginia's governor. At first, this seemed to be good news for Clark. Jefferson had long recognized the importance of the northwest, and he supported Clark's efforts there. However, Jefferson's enthusiasm for western operations was hamstrung by a lack of money. Paper money minted by Virginia and the Continental Congress was virtually worthless, and Jefferson admitted that there was little hard currency—gold or silver—available in the treasury. After just a few months, he reluctantly ordered Clark to withdraw to the eastern banks of the Ohio River in Kentucky. He had no money with which to support an army in the Illinois country.

Clark stayed in Kentucky during the bitter winter of 1779–1780, helping organize local militias. The snow was so deep that all travel was suspended. Birds fell from trees, frozen solid. Sap in maple trees froze and splintered the trees with explosive cracks that sounded like gunfire. Kentuckians called this time the Hard Winter.

Despite the lack of resources, both Jefferson and Clark wanted to hold on to the northwestern country. Jefferson ordered Clark to build a fort at the junction of the Ohio and Mississippi rivers to protect the western frontier. In April 1780, Clark began construction of Fort Jefferson on the Mississippi River at Iron Banks, five miles below the mouth of the Ohio River. It was the westernmost point in America.

The British were as determined to retake the northwest as Jefferson and Clark were to hold on to it. Early in May, the English launched their plans. They put together invading forces composed mainly of American Indians, French militia, and pro-English Americans, using Detroit as a major base of operations. One of the objectives was to seize control of the Mississippi River from the Spanish, who had come into the American Revolution on the colonial side in 1779. Another goal was to regain control of the northwest from the Americans. A third goal was to subdue Kentucky. The British force brought artillery that no Kentucky settlement could match.

The British even hoped to win control of the vitally important port of New Orleans, currently run by the Spanish and their pro-American governor, Don Bernardo de Gálvez. If the British plans succeeded, the forces attacking New Orleans and Louisiana in the south would move north up the Mississippi River and join the other groups moving down from Canada and Detroit. Then the whole group would move east.

Against these mighty hammer blows stood George Rogers Clark.

In mid-May, Clark received the first reports of what was occurring. The Spanish governor of St. Louis, Fernando de Leyba, sent him an urgent plea for assistance. A British force composed of Indians from numerous tribes was on its way to attack St. Louis and possibly American-held Cahokia across the river as a prelude to attacks up and down the Mississippi River.

At that time, St. Louis was just a tiny village with about 800 mainly French inhabitants. It was so far west, and so remote, that Virginia government officials did not know where it was located. It was nicknamed Pancore (from the French *pain court*, meaning "bread shortage") because the village was always short of food.

Although the distance between Clark and Cahokia/St. Louis was over 100 miles, Clark immediately set out for them via the Mississippi River with as many men as he could take from Fort Jefferson. He and his men had to pole and row their boats upstream against the swift Mississippi current. It was a race to see which side got there first: the enemy or Clark. Clark just barely won. He got to the area on May 25, one day before the British forces attacked. Clark was the first American government representative to ever visit St. Louis. After a hasty conference with the governor, he went over to Cahokia.

The British attacks began on May 26, 1780, but a lot of steam was taken out of the assaults when the Indians discovered that the famous and feared Long Knife was among the defenders. The Indians thought he was still at the Falls of the Ohio. Both attacks were repulsed with little or no loss of life.

Once the attacks failed, the Indians retreated. Clark sent out a group of Spanish, French, and American soldiers to pursue them. This force chased the Indians all the way back to the Michigan region.

Meanwhile, Clark had other pressing matters. He had learned that Fort Jefferson was to be attacked, so he hurried there. According to legend, this was when he pulled one of the greatest hoaxes of the war. Arriving by boat, he realized that enemy Indians were lurking in the woods all around him. He then stood up and started gesturing elaborately to what the Indians assumed were soldiers coming behind him hidden by a bend on the river.

Of course, there were no soldiers behind Clark—but the Indians waiting in ambush did not know that. For all they knew, he could have had a large force of troops right around the bend ready to attack. On the frontier, the unseen enemy was as great a threat as one that could be seen. The Indians withdrew without a shot being fired.

Meanwhile, the Indians in advance of the British force that was on its way to attack the Kentucky settlement at Louisville got word that Clark was back from the Illinois country and in Kentucky. Perhaps he was waiting for them right now.

This news brought the Indian advance to a screeching halt. They had not counted on facing Clark; they were respectful and scared of him. For two days they debated the wisdom of attacking Louisville if Clark was there. They decided against it. After attacking a few smaller Kentucky settlements, the whole British force returned to Detroit.

Indian attacks against Kentucky still concerned Clark. He knew they would not stop unless they were forced to stop. The words of Governor Jefferson rang in his ears: ". . . the same world would scarcely do for them and us."[2]

Clark rode to Harrodsburg in Kentucky to raise an army against the Shawnee tribe. When he got there, he found the men more interested in filing claims for land than in fighting Indians. Without the legal authority to do so, Clark closed the land office. Shortly he had an army of 1,000 men. It was the largest American force ever assembled beyond the Appalachian Mountains. On August 2, 1780, they set out for the Shawnee villages of Chillicothe and Piqua in what is now the state of Ohio.

This army made so much noise as it approached Chillicothe that it alerted the Shawnee. They abandoned their village so quickly that food was found still boiling over fires. The army burned the town and cut down the corn growing nearby.

At Piqua the Indians and the colonials fought a vicious battle that ended with Clark victorious. He and his men then spent the next two days there, burning hundreds of acres of corn.

As long as Detroit remained in British hands, the western frontier was in danger of attack from Indians and British troops. Realizing this, on Christmas Day, 1780, Jefferson authorized a new expedition by Clark against Detroit. He promoted Clark to brigadier general, and hoped for an advance to start around March 15.

The colonial general Benedict Arnold went over to the British side during the war. His landing and harassment of eastern Virginia in 1781 would have great consequences for Clark.

Clark's plans had to be changed quickly when Benedict Arnold, now openly on the British side, landed in Virginia with 1,600 English troops and occupied Richmond on January 5, 1781. In the confusion, the vouchers Clark had used to authorize expenditures disappeared. Although he could not have known it at the time, Arnold had destroyed Clark's future.

Clark rushed east as part of a unit of 240 Virginians under the command of Baron Friedrich von Steuben. It was the only time Clark fought in the east during the American Revolution. They met the enemy at Hood's Ferry on the James River. Although they fought gamely, the Americans were forced to withdraw.

Jefferson, still convinced that defending the frontier was the greatest need, ordered Clark back to Pittsburgh on January 22. The threat in eastern Virginia increased. Jefferson resigned as governor on June 3. Now Virginians, constantly waiting for an attack to come from the west, had to worry about attacks from the east as well.

It was a situation that would start the long, slow decline of George Rogers Clark.

Oliver Pollock

History is filled with examples of important people who have faded into its dusty pages until they are no more than a footnote. Unfortunately, that fate has befallen Oliver Pollock, financier and supplier of the American Revolution in the West.

Born in Ireland in 1737, Pollock came to America in 1760 and settled in Pennsylvania. In the late 1760s he moved to New Orleans and became one of the most important traders in the region, amassing a fortune of $100,000 by the beginning of 1776. (This was an enormous sum at that time in America.)

When the Revolutionary War broke out, Pollock began trying to win support for the American cause with Spanish officials in New Orleans. He cleverly played on Spanish fears of a British invasion of Cuba, Mexico, and New Orleans (all Spanish possessions) if England defeated the colonies.

In 1778, Pollock was instructed by the Commercial Committee of the Continental Congress to give all possible assistance to the campaign of George Rogers Clark, who was trying to secure the Northwest Territory (Indiana, Ohio, and Illinois) against the British. From Clark came a seemingly endless supply of bills that he charged to Pollock, such as: $216 for boat linens; $1,351 for 12,000 pounds of flour; $30 for a boat anchor; $10 for four pair of handcuffs; and $57 for hospital supplies.[3] Pollock dutifully assumed responsibility for it all, although it drained his fortune.

Spanish Milled Dollar, a popular form of
currency during the Revolutionary War

By the close of 1781, Pollock was in a hopeless financial situation. Destitute, suits against him for bills for which he had assumed responsibility multiplied. Eventually he was able to repay his debts, and he once again accumulated money and property. He died in December 1823.

For Your Information

Joseph Brant, a Mohawk chief, befriended the British. He was educated in a British school in Connecticut, fought for the British in the French and Indian War, and joined the Anglican Church. Around 1776, the Iroquois Confederacy named him war chief, and the British Army appointed him captain in charge of Indian forces.

CHAPTER
5

Bitter Years

In January 1781, Clark found Pittsburgh in chaos. The British, instead of organizing a formal western invasion, had instead encouraged their Indian allies to launch more numerous and vicious attacks against frontier settlements. The Indians, who wanted revenge for the attacks on Chillicothe and Piqua, needed little encouragement. Worse, another Indian tribe—the Delaware—had joined the other hostile groups, making them even stronger. Attacks against colonial settlements raged up and down the frontier. A letter written in April that year describes the horrible situation on the frontier: "We are all obliged to live in Forts in this Country . . . Whole families are destroyed. . . . Infants are torn from their mothers Arms & their Brains dashed out against Trees. . . ."[1]

The settlers could mount little defense. The worthlessness of Continental money, and the resultant lack of supplies, had forced the settlers to abandon many of Clark's victories, such as at Kaskaskia. Fort Jefferson was abandoned in June. Clark, it was whispered, had really accomplished nothing. The frontier was no safer.

With the British rampaging in eastern Virginia, Clark had trouble raising men for a defense of the west. His task became even more difficult when the Virginia assembly voted on June 21, 1781, to abandon the frontier expedition.

Clark pieced together a tiny army of 400 soldiers. A group of Pennsylvania militia was supposed to join him, but on August 8 Clark set off before they arrived. Men were deserting from his army, and Clark needed to get started before more left. The Pennsylvania militia followed him. On August 24, before they caught up to Clark, the militia was attacked by a group of Indians led by Mohawk Chief Joseph Brant. The militia was destroyed; more than 100 were killed or captured. Some people blamed Clark for the disaster.

From September 5 to 7, Clark held a series of war councils to decide whether or not to go forward with the attack on Detroit. Eventually it was decided to go on the defensive; the Detroit offensive was postponed. A discouraged Clark said, ". . . my chain appears to have run out."[2]

Even more serious were reports that Clark was drinking. The rumors had first started during the construction of Fort Jefferson, but now they got more frequent, and it appears they were true. A man wrote that Clark "has lost the confidence of the people and it is said become a sot [drunk]; perhaps something worse."[3]

The British surrender at Yorktown in October 1781 ended the fighting in the east, but the violence continued and even increased in the west. The entire Ohio Valley was burning with violence and hatred, as settlers and Indians attacked each other without mercy. On the western frontier, 1782 became known as the Year of Sorrow because of the continuing, savage violence. Some held Clark responsible: Kentucky was obviously no safer after his efforts.

In November 1782, Clark and 1,000 men spent a week burning Shawnee villages and fields. With so many of their crops destroyed, the Indians were forced to hunt more for food. The wild game in the Ohio Valley, once so plentiful, virtually vanished.

On September 3, 1783, America signed the Treaty of Paris with Britain, formally ending the Revolution. The English turned over the entire northwest to America. Some people have argued that Clark's victories were meaningless, since so much violence occurred in the region afterward. However, by repeatedly defeating the English, he had prevented Britain from trying to claim that land at the bargaining table when the peace treaty was being negotiated.

For the Indian tribes that had sided with the British, the treaty was a disaster. At the stroke of a pen, the British had signed away their land to the Americans. The Indians protested that the English had given away land that was not theirs to give, but their words fell on deaf ears. Many Shawnee and Delaware reluctantly left their ancient homes for Spanish territory in what is today Missouri.

Just thirty years old, George Rogers Clark found himself a general without an army. The western frontier was quieting down. Now he had to get ready to fight another type of battle: the battle to get paid and to be reimbursed for the many vouchers he had authorized.

Government officials who tried to figure out who and what needed to be paid were engulfed in a sea of confusion. Clark and others on the frontier were fighters, not accountants. They were usually more concerned with trying to stay alive than with proper recordkeeping. To make matters worse for Clark, his vouchers had been misplaced, so he had no official records to document his claims. He had charged $20,000 in supplies and other goods to his own credit, confident that Virginia would eventually reimburse him. It never did.

Even when the findings were in his favor, Clark did not benefit. It was officially found that he had received no pay while in the service of Virginia for four years. While thanking him for the "very great and singular services you have rendered,"[4] Virginia never paid him. Instead, the assembly passed a resolution accusing certain officers in the western country of waste and misuse of funds. Clark felt the resolution was aimed at him.

Eventually Clark received land, not cash, from the state. The land was supposedly equal to the amount of money he had spent. However, this land was swallowed up by creditors as repayment.

On July 2, 1783, Virginia's governor removed Clark from command. Since there would be no more Indian campaigns, there was no need for a brigadier general on the western frontier.

Virginia did eventually grant some land across the Ohio River from Louisville, Kentucky, to Clark and the men who had served with him in Illinois. (This was after Clark's first land grant had been taken by creditors.) The entire Clark family prepared to move.

In late December 1783, Clark received a letter from Thomas Jefferson. Jefferson had learned that England was getting ready to explore the country between the Mississippi River and California. He had been trying to organize a similar expedition. He asked Clark to lead it. Clark turned him down because he could not afford public service any longer. He needed to make money. (Years later, as president, Jefferson asked Meriwether Lewis and Clark's younger brother William to lead the expedition.)

In the spring of 1784, Clark made final preparations for his family's move to Kentucky. Indian attacks in the area were continuing, but they could not stop the influx of settlers. The population of colonial settlers in Kentucky jumped from 30,000 in 1783 to 50,000 by 1787.

The Clark family arrived in Louisville in the spring of 1785 and settled on the south fork of Beargrass Creek. They built a two-story house they named Mulberry Hill. George did some surveying and also entered into a deal to supply game to the rapidly growing town of Louisville. It failed, however, because wild game had been driven out of the area. He also served as Chairman of the Board of Commissioners for handing out lands in Illinois.

Indian attacks in Kentucky were steadily growing more numerous. The British had not abandoned some of their outposts in the northwest, as they had promised, and they were again encouraging the Indians in their attacks. In addition, the Shawnee had never accepted the decision of other tribes to sign away their land. Confusion over which tribe spoke for others prevented unified peace agreements from being implemented.

Clark tried twice in 1785 to negotiate a peace treaty with the Shawnee, but failed. In January 1786 the Shawnee attended another conference, loudly protesting the Americans' hunger for land. "God gave us this country! It is all ours!"[5] they proclaimed. Clark contemptuously ground a Shawnee wampum belt under his heel, a deliberate insult that made the Indians realize he was deadly serious about arriving at an agreement or going back to war. They signed a treaty on February 1, 1786, but it quickly collapsed. Indian attacks increased throughout the summer.

In September 1786, Clark was persuaded to take command of a group of 1,200 militia at the Falls of the Ohio. A dual attack by Clark's army and another was planned against the Shawnee. However, supply shortages and poor discipline caused many of his men to desert. The men remaining were not nearly enough, and Clark's campaign dissolved in bitterness and failure. Clark made a serious error when he took needed supplies from a group of Spanish merchants. As it

turned out, only a military commander could legally confiscate supplies. Clark had no military ranking. Lawsuits for the amount of loss suffered by the merchants followed, adding to Clark's troubles.

Clark realized he was facing financial ruin. Creditors and speculators who had bought up the notes he had personally endorsed buried him with lawsuits, seeking to force him to pay. Clark was trapped in a vicious cycle. If he went into business to make money, his creditors would seize everything. On the other hand, going into business and making money was the only way Clark could get out from under the mountain of debt—none of which was personally his, but all of which he had assumed on behalf of Virginia and his military expeditions.

Overwhelmed by the hopelessness of it all, Clark turned more than ever to alcohol. On April 19, 1787, an army paymaster wrote: "Saw Genl Clark, who is still more of a sot [drunk] than ever, not company scarcely for a beast; his character, which was once so great, is now entirely gone with the people in this country."[6] Good news was so infrequent for Clark that when Thomas Jefferson praised him in a letter to a friend, Clark saw the words and cried.

Slowly Clark sank into a pit of alcohol and despair. There was a brief interlude in the early 1790s when he became involved in a scheme to campaign against the Spanish on the Mississippi on behalf of the French. However, the federal government squashed the venture. After that, Clark just sat in his parents' house at Mulberry Hill and watched his younger brother Billy eclipse him. As his parents got older and then died, Billy was the one who settled the estates and tried mightily to help his brother get out of debt. Billy bought land belonging to George so that creditors could not seize it.

After his parents died, Clark spent his days mainly wandering the garden at Mulberry Hill. In 1803 the house was sold and Clark moved across the river to the town of Clarksville, Indiana. It was the only land he had left. He built a cabin. By this time brother Billy was accompanying Meriwether Lewis on the epic Lewis and Clark Expedition, and, except for the company of his three slaves, George Rogers Clark lived alone in his cabin.

In 1805 a visitor reported that the frail Clark was almost helpless. Early in 1809 Clark had a stroke, fell into the stone fireplace at his cabin, and badly burned his leg. The burns did not heal, and

Meriwether Lewis co-led the famous Lewis & Clark Expedition across western America. His partner was William Clark, the younger brother of George Rogers Clark.

amputation was required. Clark requested that a military band play outside his window while the amputation—without anesthetic, which had not yet been invented—was being performed.

After he recovered from the operation, he stayed with his sister Lucy and her husband at Locust Grove, near Louisville. Much of his body became paralyzed, and he spent most of his time in a large, rolling armchair. About 1812, Virginia voted him a yearly pension of $400 and a sword of honor. Reportedly, after the assembly voted him these awards, the members were so moved by Clark's pitiful condition that they broke down in tears.

On February 13, 1818, George Rogers Clark, who had saved the American West, died in Locust Grove at the age of sixty-six. Almost 100 years later, his account books that detailed every expense of his campaigns and proved to the penny what he had spent were found in a dusty storage room in Richmond, Virginia.

A Hero Ignored and Eclipsed

George Rogers Clark played a critical part in safeguarding the western frontier, and in the overall outcome of the revolution itself. But unlike other Revolutionary War figures, Clark's actions were virtually ignored, and he has not been considered as one of America's founding figures. Why?

Some feel there are several reasons that Clark's accomplishments are often overlooked:

1. At the time of the war, the main area of concern was the east and how Washington's army was faring. Not many people placed the same importance on the west and the critical role that the Northwest Territory would play in the future growth of America. Even today, far more emphasis is given to Washington and his troops compared to Clark.

2. Communication was slow in those days. Many people in the east did not hear about Clark's deeds. He was a hero to those living on the frontier, but unknown elsewhere.

3. The people who organized the slander and lies campaign about him in order to discredit him in Kentucky did a good job.

William Clark

Ironically, it was Clark's younger brother William who ultimately achieved fame as coleader of the Lewis and Clark Expedition. William Clark was chosen for the assignment after a distinguished military career. On the historic trip, he served as the expedition's chief mapmaker and diplomat to the many Native Americans encountered along the way.

In May 1804, Lewis, Clark, and nearly four dozen men set out from St. Louis. Sailing, canoeing, and hiking, they followed the Missouri River north and west to Iowa, then across the Great Divide, and down the Columbia River. Having traveled over 4,100 miles, in November 1805 they came to within a few miles of the Pacific Ocean, camped for the winter, and began the return trip in March.

The trip made William Clark famous. After Meriwether Lewis's untimely death in 1809, Clark completed the group's final report. He also was influential in Native American affairs. He died in 1838—certainly the more renowned of the Clark brothers.

For Your Information

Chronology

1752	George Rogers Clark is born in Albemarle County, Virginia
1757	Clark family moves to a plantation in Caroline County, Virginia
1764	George and his brother Jonathan reportedly go to a school run by Donald Robertson
1770	George's youngest brother, William, is born
1772–1774	Clark explores the Ohio River Valley
1774	Attacks by Indians and whites against each other increase in Ohio River Valley (spring); in May, Clark receives first military commission as captain of the Pittsburgh militia
1775	As deputy surveyor for Ohio Company, Clark surveys what is now state of Kentucky in the spring. In the autumn he returns to Virginia to find out about claims in Kentucky
1776	Clark returns to Kentucky and becomes a military and political leader; with John Gabriel Jones, leaves for Virginia to ask for aid for campaign in the west
1777	Is promoted to major of Virginia militia
1778	In January, receives permission from Virginia legislature and Governor Patrick Henry for western campaign; establishes Fort Nelson; is promoted to lieutenant colonel; in July–August, takes British outposts of Kaskaskia and Vincennes; in December, British retake Vincennes
1779	Leaves Kaskaskia on February 5 for march of nearly 200 miles to retake Vincennes; Vincennes surrenders February 25
1779–1782	Builds forts and leads military expeditions against Indians in defense of Kentucky
1780	Is promoted to brigadier general
1781	Virginia gives up claims to all lands northwest of the Ohio River and discontinues support for Clark's militia and forts
1782	"The Year of Sorrow"; Clark and his men burn Shawnee villages and fields
1783	Virginia relieves Clark of his military command; Clark and his men receive 150,000 acres of land by Virginia
1784	Board of Commissioners meets in Louisville to settle land claims and other matters relating to Clark and his men
1785	Clark family home is established at Mulberry Hill, Louisville; George begins surveying again
1803	Clark builds his own cabin on Clark Point, Clarksville, Indiana
1809	Clark has a stroke and burns his leg, which has to be amputated
1812	Virginia grants him a yearly pension
1818	Dies at Locust Grove, near Louisville, on February 13

Timeline in History

1705	Edmund Halley predicts the frequency of visits by Halley's comet.
1707	England and Scotland unite to create Great Britain.
1714	Britain's Queen Anne dies.
1715	First folding umbrella debuts in Paris.
1718	New Orleans is founded.
1727	Sir Isaac Newton dies.
1731	Benjamin Franklin begins a circulating library in Philadelphia.
1752	Benjamin Franklin performs his kite and lightning experiment.
1754	French and Indian War begins in North America between England and France.
1763	Treaty ends French and Indian War. England gains all land east of Mississippi River except New Orleans.
1765–1768	Approximately 30,000 people settle west of the Appalachian Mountains.
1762	New York City hosts its first St. Patrick's Day parade.
1769	Napoléon Bonaparte is born.
1775	American Revolution starts with the Battle of Lexington.
1776	Declaration of Independence is issued.
1781	Cornwallis surrenders to Washington at Yorktown.
1789	The French Revolution begins.
1796	George Washington gives his farewell address.
1803	President Thomas Jefferson concludes the Louisiana Purchase.
1807	Robert E. Lee is born.
1809	Abraham Lincoln is born.
1812	War of 1812 is declared.
1815	Napoléon Bonaparte is defeated at Waterloo.
1821	First American colonists go to Texas.
1827	Ludwig van Beethoven dies.
1828	Noah Webster writes the *American Dictionary of the English Language.*
1836	Texas freedom fighters are defeated at the Battle of the Alamo.
1837	Samuel B. Morse invents the telegraph.
1845	Edgar Allen Poe writes "The Raven."
1847	Thomas A. Edison is born.
1848	Gold is discovered in California.
1849	First chocolate bar is unveiled.

Chapter Notes

Chapter 1   Critical Crossing

1. *The American Heritage Book of the Revolution* (New York: American Heritage Publishing Company, Inc., 1958), p. 302.

Chapter 2   Early Life

1. John Bakeless, *Background to Glory—The Life of George Rogers Clark* (Philadelphia: J. B. Lippincott Company, 1957), p. 31.

2. Dale Van Every, *A Company of Heroes—The American Frontier* (New York: William Morrow and Company, 1962), p. 81.

3. Bakeless, p. 41.

Chapter 3   Long Knives

1. John Bakeless, *Background to Glory—The Life of George Rogers Clark* (Philadelphia: J. B. Lippincott Company, 1957), p. 56.

2. Landon Y. Jones, *William Clark and the Shaping of the West* (New York: Hill and Wang, 2004), p. 35.

3. Ibid., p. 35.

4. Ibid., p. 36.

5. Ibid., p. 36.

6. Bakeless, p. 148.

7. Jones, p. 37.

8. Ibid., p. 38.

Chapter 4   Opportunity Lost

1. Dale Van Every, *A Company of Heroes—The American Frontier* (New York: William Morrow and Company, 1962), p. 196.

2. Landon Y. Jones, *William Clark and the Shaping of the West* (New York: Hill and Wang, 2004), p. 40.

3. James Alton James, *Oliver Pollock* (Freeport, New York: Books for Libraries Press, 1937), p. 141.

Chapter 5   Bitter Years

1. Dale Van Every, *A Company of Heroes—The American Frontier* (New York: William Morrow and Company, 1962), p. 255.

2. Ibid., p. 263.

3. Landon Y. Jones, *William Clark and the Shaping of the West* (New York: Hill and Wang, 2004), p. 43.

4. John Bakeless, *Background to Glory—The Life of George Rogers Clark* (Philadelphia: J. B. Lippincott Company, 1957), p. 309.

5. Jones, p. 53.

6. Bakeless, p. 336.

Further Reading

For Young Adults

Markley, Helen Miller. *George Rogers Clark, Frontier Fighter.* New York: Putnam, 1968.

Lee, Susan. *George Rogers Clark: War in the West.* Chicago: Childrens Press, 1975.

Havinghurst, Walter. *George Rogers Clark, Soldier in the West.* New York: McGraw-Hill, 1952.

De Leeuw, Adele. *George Rogers Clark; Frontier Fighter.* Champaign, Illinois: Gerrard Publishing Co., 1967.

Works Consulted

The American Heritage Book of the Revolution. New York: American Heritage Publishing Co., Inc., 1958.

Bakeless, John. *Background to Glory—The Life of George Rogers Clark.* Philadelphia: J. B. Lippincott Company, 1957.

Countryman, Edward. *The American Revolution.* New York: Hill and Wang, 1985.

James, James Alton. *Oliver Pollock.* Freeport, New York: Books for Libraries Press, 1937.

Jones, Landon Y. *William Clark and the Shaping of the West.* New York: Hill and Wang, 2004.

Middlekauff, Robert. *The Glorious Cause: The American Revolution, 1763–1789.* New York: Oxford University Press, 1982.

Thom, James Alexander. *Long Knife.* New York: Avon Books, 1979.

Van Every, Dale. *A Company of Heroes—The American Frontier.* New York: William Morrow and Company, 1962.

On the Internet

The Chronicles of George Rogers Clark
http://www.wfpl.org/grc/archive.htm

George Rogers Clark National Historical Park
http://www.nps.gov/gero/home.html

Indiana Historical Bureau, George Rogers Clark biography
http://www.statelib.lib.in.us/WWW/IHB/resources/grcbio.html

Locust Grove: About George Rogers Clark
http://www.locustgrove.org/aboutgrc.html

Kentucky Department for Libraries and Archives: "George Rogers Clark: Kentucky Frontiersman, Hero, and Founder of Louisville"
http://www.kdla.ky.gov/resources/kygrclark.htm

Index